BLOCKCHAIN

Understand the Revolutionary Digital
Economy of the Future

PETER VAN DIJCK

Copyright Notice.

©Peter van Dijck

All rights reserved. No part of this publication may be reproduced, distributed or transmitted by any means or in any form, including but not limited to photocopying, recording, or other electronic or mechanical methods, without the prior written permission of the publisher, except in the case of brief quotations embodied in reviews and certain noncommercial uses acceptable to the copyright law.

Trademarked names appear in an editorial style without trademark symbols accompanying every occurrence of trademark names throughout the eBook. These names are used with no intention to infringe on the copyrights of respective owner trademarks. The information in this book is distributed on an "as is" basis, exclusively for educational purposes, without warranty. Neither the author nor the publisher shall have any liability to any person or entity with respect to any loss or damage caused or alleged to be caused directly or indirectly by the information contained in this book.

By reading this document, the reader agrees that Peter van Dijck is under no circumstances responsible for any losses, direct or indirect, which are incurred as a result of the use of information contained within this document, including, but not limited to, — errors, omissions or inaccuracies.

Table of Contents

CHAPTER1: INTRODUCTION TO BLOCKCHAIN 1

CHAPTER 2: BLOCKCHAIN TECHNOLOGY 11

CHAPTER 3: BLOCKCHAIN HISTORY 16

CHAPTER 4: BLOCKCHAIN PRESS 20

CHAPTER 5: BLOCKCHAIN NEWS 27

CHAPTER 6: BLOCKCHAIN INVENTION 32

CHAPTER 7: BLOCKCHAIN REMITTANCE 39

CHAPTER 8: BLOCKCHAIN SOFTWARE 45

CHAPTER1: INTRODUCTION TO BLOCKCHAIN

In the simplest terms, a blockchain is a digital ledger of transactions, not unlike the ledgers we have been using for hundreds of years to record sales and purchases. The function of this digital ledger is, in fact, nearly identical to a traditional ledger in that it records debits and credits between people. That is the core concept behind blockchain; the difference is who holds the ledger and who verifies the transactions.

With traditional transactions, a payment from one person to another involves some kind of intermediary to facilitate the transaction. Let's say David wants to transfer £20 to OZ. He can either give her cash in the form of a £20 note, or he can use some banking app to transfer the money directly to her bank account. In both cases, a bank is an intermediary verifying the transaction: David funds are verified when he takes the money out of a cash machine, or they are verified by the app when he makes the digital transfer. The bank decides if the transaction should go ahead. The bank also holds the record of all transactions made by David and is solely responsible for updating it whenever David pays someone or receives money into his account. In other words, the bank holds and controls the ledger, and everything flows through the bank.

That's a lot of responsibility, so it's important that David feels he can trust his bank otherwise he would not risk his money with them. He needs to feel confident that the bank will not defraud him, will not lose his money, will not be robbed, and will not disappear overnight. This need for trust had underpinned virtually every major behavior and facet of the monolithic finance industry, to the extent that even when it was discovered that banks were being irresponsible with our money during the financial crisis of 2008.

The government (another intermediary) chose to bail them out rather than risk destroying the final fragments of trust by letting them collapse.

Blockchains operate differently in one key respect: they are entirely decentralized. There is no central clearing house like a bank, and there is no central ledger held by one entity. Instead, the ledger is distributed across a vast network of computers, called nodes, each of which holds a copy of the entire ledger on their respective hard drives. These nodes are connected to one another via a piece of software called a peer-to-peer (P2P) client, which synchronizes data across the network of nodes and makes sure that everybody has the same version of the ledger at any given point in time.

When a new transaction is entered into a blockchain, it is first encrypted using state-of-the-art cryptographic technology. Once encrypted, the transaction is converted to something called a block, which is the term used for an encrypted group of new transactions. That block is then sent (or broadcast) into the network of computer nodes, where it is verified by the nodes and, once verified, passed on through the network so that the block can be added to the end of the ledger on everybody's computer, under the list of all previous blocks. This is called the chain. Hence the tech is referred to as a blockchain.

Once approved and recorded into the ledger, the transaction can be completed. This is how crypto currencies like Bitcoin work.

Accountability and the removal of trust

What are the advantages of this system over a banking or central clearing system? Why would Rob use Bitcoin instead of normal currency?

BLOCKCHAIN

The answer is trust. As mentioned before, with the banking system it is critical that Rob trusts his bank to protect his money and handle it properly. To ensure this happens, enormous regulatory systems exist to verify the actions of the banks and ensure they are fit for purpose. Governments then regulate the regulators, creating a sort of tiered system of checks whose sole purpose is to help prevent mistakes and bad behavior. In other words, organizations like the Financial Services Authority exist precisely because banks can't be trusted on their own. And banks frequently make mistakes and misbehave, as we have seen too many times. When you have a single source of authority, power tends to get abused or misused. The trust relationship between people and banks is awkward and precarious: we don't really trust them but we don't feel there is much alternative.

Blockchain systems, on the other hand, don't need you to trust them at all. All transactions (or blocks) in a blockchain are verified by the nodes in the network before being added to the ledger, which means there is no single point of failure and no single approval channel. If a hacker wanted to successfully tamper with the ledger on a blockchain, they would have to simultaneously hack millions of computers, which is almost impossible. A hacker would also be pretty much unable to bring a blockchain network down, as, again, they would need to be able to shut down every single computer in a network of computers distributed around the world.

The encryption process itself is also a key factor. Blockchains like the Bitcoin one use deliberately difficult processes for their verification procedure. In the case of Bitcoin, blocks are verified by nodes performing a deliberate processor- and time-intensive series of calculations, often in the form of puzzles or complex mathematical problems, which mean that verification is neither instant nor accessible. Nodes that do commit the resource to verification of blocks are rewarded with a transaction fee and a bounty of newly-minted Bitcoins. This has the function of both incentivizing people to become nodes (because processing blocks like this require pretty powerful computers and a lot of electricity), while also handling the process of generating - or minting - units of the currency. This is referred to as mining because it involves a considerable amount of effort (by a computer, in this case) to produce a new commodity. It also means that transactions are verified by the most independent way possible, more independent than a government-regulated organization like the FSA.

This decentralized, democratic and highly secure nature of blockchains means that they can function without the need for regulation (they are self-regulating), government or another opaque intermediary. They work because people don't trust each other, rather than in spite of.

Let the significance of that sink in for a while, and the excitement around blockchain starts to make sense.

Smart contracts

Where things get interesting is the applications of blockchain beyond crypto currencies like Bitcoin. Given that one of the underlying principles of the blockchain system is the secure, independent verification of a transaction, it's easy to imagine other ways in which this type of process can be valuable. Unsurprisingly, many such applications are already in use or development. Some of the best ones are:

Smart contracts (Ethereum): probably the most exciting blockchain development after Bitcoin, smart contracts are blocks that contain code that must be executed for the contract to be fulfilled. The code can be anything, as long as a computer can execute it, but in simple terms, it means that you can use blockchain technology (with its independent verification, trustless architecture and security) to create a kind of escrow system for any transaction. As an example, if you're a web designer you could create a contract that verifies if a new client's website is launched or not, and then automatically release the funds to you once it is. No more chasing or invoicing. Smart contracts are also being used to prove ownership of an asset such as property or art. The potential for reducing fraud with this approach is enormous.

Cloud storage (Store): cloud computing has revolutionized the web and brought about the advent of Big Data which has, in turn, kick-started the new AI revolution. But most cloud-based systems are run on servers stored in single-location server farms, owned by a single entity (Amazon, Rackspace, Google, etc.). This presents all the same problems as the banking system, in that your data is controlled by a single, opaque organization which represents a single point of failure. Distributing data on a blockchain removes the trust issue entirely and also promises to increase reliability as it is so much harder to take a blockchain network down.

Digital identification (ShoCard): two of the biggest issues of our time are identified theft and data protection. With vast centralized services such as Facebook holding so much data about us, and efforts by various developed-world governments to store digital information about their citizens in a central database, the potential for abuse of our data is terrifying. Blockchain technology offers a potential solution to this by wrapping your key data up into an encrypted block that can be verified by the blockchain network whenever you need to prove your identity. The applications of this range from the obvious replacement of passports and I.D. cards to other areas such as replacing passwords. It could be huge.

Digital voting: highly topical in the wake of the investigation into Russia's influence on the recent U.S. election, digital voting has long been suspected of being both unreliable and highly vulnerable to tampering. Blockchain technology offers a way of verifying that a voter's vote was successfully sent while retaining their anonymity. It promises not only to reduce fraud in elections but also to increase general voter turnout as people will be able to vote on their mobile phones.

Blockchain technology is still very much in its infancy, and most of the applications are a long way from general use. Even Bitcoin, the most established blockchain platform, is subject to huge volatility indicative of its relative newcomer status. However, the potential for blockchain to solve some of the major problems we face today makes it an extraordinarily exciting and seductive technology to follow.

One of the most talked-about topics in the financial services industry today is blockchain. If fully adopted, it will enable banks to process payments more quickly and more accurately while reducing transaction processing costs and the requirement for exceptions.

However, to capitalize on this potential, banks need to build the infrastructure required to create and operate a true global network using solutions based on this transformative technology.

A global network is critical to helping banks use blockchain to help transform payments at scale and help reduce risk of failure. The most effective network should have two defining characteristics:

1. It should include the necessary defined rights, obligations, controls, and standards.
2. It should offer a quick and efficient onboarding process that enables banks to essentially "plug and play" into the network for both existing and future corridors.

Blockchain and distributed ledgers have a bright future. As real-time, open-source and trusted platforms that securely transmit data and value, they can help banks not only reduce the cost of processing payments, but also create new products and services that can generate important new revenue streams.

The biggest key to turning blockchain's potential into reality is a collaborative effort among banks to create the network necessary to support global payments. Banks need to look at the bigger picture and work together — and with non-banks — to help define the backbone that can underpin a universally accepted, ubiquitous global payment system that can transform how banks execute transactions.

ELEMENTS OF BLOCKCHAIN

Decentralization: Rather than one central authority controlling everything within an ecosystem, blockchain distributes control among all peers in the transaction chain, creating a shared infrastructure.

Digital signature: Blockchain enables an exchange of transactional value using unique digital signatures that rely on public keys (decryption code known to everyone on the network) and private keys (codes known only to the owner) to create proof of ownership.

Mining: A distributed consensus system rewards miners for confirmation and verification of transactions and stores them in blocks using strict cryptographic rules.

Data integrity: The use of complex algorithms and consensus among users ensures that transaction data, once agreed upon, cannot be tampered with. Data stored on blockchain thus acts as a single version of truth for all parties involved, reducing the risk of fraud.

Implementing Blockchain Despite the heightened activity over the past year or so, it is still very early days for blockchain. Banks' blockchain initiatives are at various stages of internal trials. Changes incurred by blockchain, such as storing data in multiple locations rather than one central location, represent a radical shift in the way banks operate. This in itself could be a major hurdle to overcome in terms of organizational culture.

Nevertheless, given its disruptive potential, banks would be advised not to begin taking steps toward incorporating blockchain into their existing systems. What follows are a subset of the key initial steps banks should consider when implementing a blockchain platform alongside existing systems.

STEPS OF IMPLEMENTING BLOCKCHAIN

Identify opportunities for innovation

The key question to ask before starting a trial is which processes to move to blockchain. This can be tricky. Blockchain is essentially a shared database, and banks have commonly relied on database management technologies to store and control access to data. Creating a working group that explores the pros and cons of moving a process to blockchain would be an ideal place to start. Such a group would operate like a startup and explore areas where blockchain can add value, while staying in sync with the bank's strategic goals.

Assess feasibility and impact on existing systems.

This involves weighing the benefits Changes incurred by blockchain, such as storing data in multiple locations rather than one central location, represent a radical shift in the way banks operate. And costs of moving a process to blockchain. Taking the perspective of key stakeholders and partners impacted by the move is critical.

Test proofs of concept

Not all ideas will have the potential to reach this stage, but once a proof-of-concept (PoC) application is ready, it needs to be tested against real-world simulations to identify areas of improvement. By measuring the results against expectations, banks will be able to refine the application and use this knowledge for future application development

Understand the regulatory environment and data security

External factors such as regulations play an important role in the blockchain era. The current regulatory framework has no provisions for accommodating a technology that could eliminate intermediaries. Storing customer data on computers in different countries will also require banks compliance with data privacy laws that may vary from one country to another. Similarly, there is no framework of regulations to make smart contracts work in the capital markets as they exist today.

CHAPTER 2: BLOCKCHAIN TECHNOLOGY

People all over the world are talking about the hype that involves various discussions about blockchain and blockchain technology. The recent development in this field has encouraged the people and organizations that are related to different financial activities, directly or indirectly. You should also feel the pleasure by the recent report of World Economic Forum that claims that 10 percent of the world's GDP would be stored on various block chains or the blockchain technology. This claim is not a joke, and that is why everyone involved in such a business must consider this assertion seriously. However, people all around the world are still not fully aware of the terms, and they still require some idea as of what this technology does.

The people, who understand the utilities and power of Block Chain, term it as the 'Internet of Values.' The claim may or may not be true. However, the new tech enthusiasts would need some clarification to develop an understanding of the valued technology with loads of possibilities and promise.

Sharing information and various other things through the Internet has become a part of everyday life worldwide. The same thing can be done for transferring value using the Internet. The term 'value' should be referred to as 'money' here. At present, we cannot think anything except banks and other money transfer platforms when it comes to transferring money from one account to another. PayPal has been one such platform that the users need to integrate to their bank accounts for sending or receiving money. It won't be wrong if you term the banks and other financial services as 'middle man.'

The revolutionary idea of blockchain technology does not confirm the idea of this 'middle man' anywhere. The technology is powerful enough to do the same transfer of money. The technology does everything by three separate roles, namely recording the transactions, establishing the identity, and confirming the contracts. The effectiveness of the technology can be measured by the fact the transfer is accurate, and it is faster than any other method of transferring money men have used till date.

There is no doubt that the market of financial services is the biggest and the most preferred by people from all walks of life. The blockchain technology has the power and strength to replace the financial services. It can do the same by enabling bulk and individual transactions. It has the required potential and efficiency to manage such transactions easily.

The term 'Block Chain Technology' came into existence a few years ago when it was associated with Bitcoin, the virtual currency that is also gaining popularity these days. It increases the value of the currency as well. As per the estimate, the value rose to more than $1000 between the years 2011 and 2013. This is incredible in the opinion of the experts who have a great idea for the successful operations of Blockchain Software. The world is standing on the verge of another revolution that can bring more freedom for transferring money from one account to another without using the traditional methods

Blockchain technology consists of data batches called "blocks" that use cryptographic validation to link themselves together. In other words, each block references and identifies the previous block by a hashing function (any function that can be used to map data of arbitrary size to data of fixed size), forming an unbroken chain, hence the name "Blockchain." It is a digital database, but unlike most databases, it is not stored in a single master location or managed by any particular body. Instead, it is decentralized and is replicated and synchronized via the internet and is visible to anyone within the network.

There are many advantages and benefits of using blockchain technology in the financial sector, to name a few:

Disintermediation - two parties can make an exchange without the oversight or intermediation of a third party such as banks and governments, with the users having total control of all their information and transactions.

Durability, Reliability and Longevity - Due to decentralized networks, blockchain does not have a central point of failure and is better able to withstand malicious attacks.

Transparency - changes to public block chains are publicly viewable by all parties creating transparency and therefore massively reducing the possibility of money laundering.

Faster Transactions with Lower Transaction Costs - By eliminating third party intermediaries and overhead costs, blockchain transactions can take minutes and are processed 24/7 at much lower transaction costs.

At HYBSE, the customers are the most important visitor. They are not done a favor by providing their services; rather they are doing us a favor by giving us the opportunity to do so. This is why our development thus far has been a critical process. Having said that, we are still in the process of perfecting and finalizing the finer details before we launch the blockchain technology. It should not be long until it is fully functional. We expect it to be fully operational by the end of March 2017.

The wallet is offered free of charge, the only cost you will face is the EUR 1200.00 for the access through the depot-wallet to the Hybrid Stock Exchange. Orders can then be placed directly onto the Stock Market without any middlemen.

Some organizations and companies started working on blockchain technology and even promoting their work so that the new financial technology reaches to places. Needless to say, it must also be mentioned here for traders that there is a lot of argument about which is the best blockchain product; however, if they know all of them, it is easy for them to use one.

Similarly, when traders and investors are aware of the latest events and policy changes taking place regarding blockchain and its various products like Bitcoin and others, they are well placed to tackle the issues. Each according to his taste can though decide his option; however, the stakeholders who subscribe to the latest blockchain press release are the one placed well.

Notwithstanding that as blockchain technology will be in great shape in the next couple of years, the people who have started earlier are going to be the biggest beneficiary. Needless to say, the traders who have made money trading Bitcoin and other blockchain products believe that balance of the two is a suitable option for them and they must subscribe to releases.

Finding out Perfect Solution

With the help of blockchain press releases, the companies that are involved in the industry tend to promote their products and services with little cost. It must also be mentioned here that the blockchain is seen as the main technological innovation of Bitcoin since it stands as proof of all the transactions on the network.

Therefore, a large number of Bitcoin companies are in turn promoting blockchain technology so that their identity as the new financial technology company is boosted. Here a block is the 'current' part of a blockchain which records some or all of the recent transactions. It appears promoting the new financial technology is the idea behind it.

Promoting Blockchain Technology for Larger Interest

When the larger interest of blockchain technology comes to mind, promoting it is essential, and for the purpose blockchain press release can play a major role. A lot of new developments take place in blockchain technology that must be published for the larger interest of the people. All the stakeholders should be kept in mind while publishing such a release.

Least but not the last, whereas the blockchain is like a full history of banking transactions, blockchain press releases are vital for the historical development of the new financial technology. Conclusively, it must be added that catching an early trend needs knowing well the technology and for that subscribing to blockchain press release is a great idea.

CHAPTER 3: BLOCKCHAIN HISTORY

Historically, when it comes to transacting money or anything of value, people and businesses have relied heavily on intermediaries like banks and governments to ensure trust and certainty Middlemen perform a range of important tasks that help build trust into the transactional process like authentication & record keeping.

The need for intermediaries is especially acute when making a digital transaction. Because digital assets like money, stocks & intellectual property, are essentially files, they are incredibly easy to reproduce. This creates what's known as the double spending problem (the act of spending the same unit of value more than once) which until now has prevented the peer to peer transfer of digital assets.

But what if there was a way of conducting digital transactions without a third party intermediary? Well, a new technology exists today that makes this possible. But before we dive into the mechanics of this revolutionary technology, it's important to provide a little context.

Blockchain Vs Bitcoin — what's the connection?

Bitcoin first appeared in a 2008 white paper authored by a person, or persons using the pseudonym Satoshi Nakamoto. The white paper detailed an innovative peer to peer electronic cash system called Bitcoin that enabled online payments to be transferred directly, without an intermediary.

While the proposed bitcoin payment system was exciting and innovative, it was the mechanics of how it worked that was truly revolutionary. Shortly after the white paper's release, it became evident that the main technical innovation was not the digital currency itself but the technology that lay behind it, known today as blockchain.

Although commonly associated with Bitcoin, blockchain technology has many other applications. Bitcoin is merely the first and most well-known uses. In fact, Bitcoin is only one of about seven hundred applications that use the blockchain operating system today.

One example of the evolution and broad application of blockchain, beyond digital currency, is the development of the Ethereum public blockchain, which is providing a way to execute peer to peer contracts.

What's under the blockchain hood?

Blockchain is a type of distributed ledger or decentralized database that keeps records of digital transactions. Rather than having a central administrator like a traditional database, (think banks, governments & accountants), a distributed ledger has a network of replicated databases, synchronized via the internet and visible to anyone within the network. Blockchain networks can be private with restricted membership similar to an intranet, or public, like the Internet, accessible to any person in the world.

When a digital transaction is carried out, it is grouped together in a cryptographically protected block with other transactions that have occurred in the last 10 minutes and sent out to the entire network. Miners (members in the network with high levels of computing power) then compete to validate the transactions by solving complex coded problems. The first miner to solve the problems and validate the block receives a reward. (In the Bitcoin Blockchain network, for example, a miner would receive Bitcoins).

The validated block of transactions is then time stamped and added to a chain in a linear, chronological order. New blocks of validated transactions are linked to older blocks, making a chain of blocks that show every transaction made in the history of that blockchain. The entire chain is continually updated so that every ledger in the network is the same, giving each member the ability to prove who owns what at any given time.

Blockchain's decentralized, open & cryptographic nature allow people to trust each other and transact peer to peer, making the need for intermediaries obsolete. This also brings unprecedented security benefits. Hacking attacks that commonly impact large centralized intermediaries like banks would be virtually impossible to pull off on the blockchain. For example — if someone wanted to hack into a particular block in a blockchain, a hacker would not only need to hack into that specific block, but all of the proceeding blocks going back the entire history of that blockchain. And they would need to do it on every ledger in the network, which could be millions, simultaneously.

Will the blockchain transform the Internet & the global economy?

Make no mistake about it. Blockchain is a highly disruptive technology that promises to change the world as we know it.

By enabling the digitization of assets, blockchain is driving a fundamental shift from the Internet of information, where we can instantly view, exchange and communicate information to the Internet of value, where we can instantly exchange assets. A new global economy of immediate value transfer is on its way, where big intermediaries no longer play a major role. An economy where trust is established not by central intermediaries but through consensus and complex computer code

Blockchain has applications that go way beyond obvious things like digital currencies and money transfers. From electronic voting, smart contracts & digitally recorded property assets to patient health records management and proof of ownership for digital content.

Blockchain will profoundly disrupt hundreds of industries that rely on intermediaries, including banking, finance, academia, real estate, and insurance, legal, health care and the public sector — amongst many others. This will result in job losses and the complete transformation of entire industries. But overall, the elimination of intermediaries brings mostly positive benefits. Banks & governments for example, often impede the free flow of business because of the time it takes to process transactions and regulatory requirements. The blockchain will enable an increased amount of people and businesses to trade much more frequently and efficiently, significantly boosting local and international trade. Blockchain technology would also eliminate expensive intermediary fees that have become a burden on individuals and businesses, especially in the remittances space.

Perhaps most profoundly, blockchain promises to democratize & expand the global financial system. Giving people who have limited exposure to the global economy, better access to financial and payment systems and stronger protection against corruption and exploitation.

CHAPTER 4: BLOCKCHAIN PRESS

As the blockchain technology is reaching to the new people and new market, a lot of people have started using it. Even central banks are recommending for exploration of the technology. However, there is still need to take the technology to a large section of people, and for that blockchain, press releases can be an extremely great an idea.

Notwithstanding what a press release, a tool in a successful public relations campaign, can be extremely useful. Experts believe that blockchain press releases are the best solution when it comes to cost-effective public relations. These are very useful tool in the overall public relations arsenal that reaches to maximum people and yet at comparatively low cost.

Interestingly, blockchain press release should convey, in a concise manner, a message that is accessible to a wide variety of audiences and make the news available for other media groups. Needless to say, the release in its best form can be read by a reporter or editor who then wants to write or broadcast about the subject to their audience.

Professional Press Release Writing

To best convey the message whether it is Blockchain Company or an organization serving the people, the blockchain press release should be written by professionals. They should create a press release that would build awareness of their product. Additionally, the point should be made across in the best possible manner.

Notwithstanding what professional press release writers should do comprehensive research before writing a blockchain press release.

They should know everything they can learn about the product, the company, the spokesperson. Additionally, they should know which media outlets would be best for them to publish the news.

Blockchain Technology Promotion

Blockchain technology is emerging as an alternative to the traditional financial technology, and for that reason, a lot of interests are coming up from various quarters. Then some organizations are trying to promote the technology as it can have great potential. Using blockchain press release to promote the technology could be a great idea.

This idea that press release should be used for the greater wellness of the blockchain technology and that must be explored. The portals providing coverage to blockchain technology should be the focus of the press release writing so that they pick the story up. In a nutshell, it must be said that blockchain press releases if written well can communicate the message well.

There are dozens of advantages from press releases as these are also helpful for global publicity to a great extent with several other additional benefits for the organizations. Needless to say, as blockchain technology is catching popular attention, a lot of organizations are now looking for professional blockchain press releases for promotional and expansion purposes.

Notwithstanding what the Internet has been very instrumental in helping news to travel greater distances in a short amount of time, blockchain press releases are the extremely great solution for companies or organizations involved in the financial technology. The people who fancy about the latest financial technology tend to make the great point using this promotional method.

As it has been mentioned above there are dozens of benefits from blockchain technology, a lot of companies have started adapting it. However, once they are into it, they need to promote their services or products as well, for that there is nothing better than blockchain press releases which are being considered the most suitable for promotional purposes.

Press Releases Reach to Most People

Out of various advantages blockchain, press releases also include the fact that these are always in demand for new information and angles for news stories. Needless to say all news organizations, including magazine editors, broadcast, and industry specific editors use press releases to develop the bulk of their published news stories.

Notwithstanding what from a consumer stand point, editors who report on the blockchain press release are considered disinterested parties, meaning that the announcement was chosen because of public demand for relevant and useful information. According to experts and observers, this third party credibility is invaluable for companies.

Benefits to Sending Out News Releases Include

Not just low cost, blockchain press releases are also known for providing increased visibility for the company. The cost-benefit analysis should be done when the promotional tools are being used, and when this is done to merit, press releases come in shining colors. There are no other methods available these days that are cheaper than press releases.

Similarly, as there is high demand for press releases and they come with added credibility for the organization, a lot of organizations are willing to explore the tool. Fetching new customers and new investors as well as free publicity, blockchain press releases are the tools for generating huge publicity. Thus, there is no better promotional tool that press release for blockchain.

Ever since Bitcoin came to existence the magnanimous financial technology blockchain has been making to news stories around the world. The press has given extensive coverage to the stories that blockchain can be the next big thing in the financial technology sector. The blockchain press releases have also shown to the world that there is an alternative as well.

Needless to say, Bitcoin press releases have also been cardinal part of the promotion of blockchain technology as it is the most popular product from blockchain. Notwithstanding what press release distribution services are industry-specific and ensure location targeting. This feature makes it extremely useful idea or strategy for organizations.

It must be noted that a prominent advantage that increases your odds of promoting your message to all is using blockchain press releases is that you are reaching to all sorts of people. Some experts believe that in front of an audience that is more likely to respond to your CTAs such strategies tend to work well.

Reaching to New Target and Solutions

Blockchain press releases are the solution that can often be used for promoting the businesses and organizations. There are professional services providers for this job that charge handsome amount. Interestingly, this type of services based on geographical location can maximize your reach and acquire new people or customers as well.

Similarly, the latest and updated blockchain press releases help you get in touch with people who share your vision, mission and interests and would be more inclined to test, buy and recommend your products. Notwithstanding what with the help of these press releases new people are brought into the fold for better.

Look for the Perfect Occasion to Distribute Your Blockchain press releases

Experts also claim that when any person is striving to make a name in an overcrowded market, it is vital to explore all available mediums. The same maxim applies in blockchain based organizations as well. Therefore, it is important to understand that blockchain press releases are not just shared but also promoted for better output.

Needless to say, blockchain press releases ensure media coverage and can help you see your story in newspapers. Additionally, magazines can also cover the story and make the entire affair popular. The blockchain press releases written by professional writers and promoted by the best brains can be extremely successful. However, for that actions must be on track.

If you are running a business, you can take advantage of press releases; this is a traditional method that has long been in use. However, ever since crypto currencies came into existence some companies that are dealing in Bitcoin, Dog coin, lite coin, ripple, etc. the role for blockchain press releases have gone up.

BLOCKCHAIN

Needless to say, you can now pay for writing, and promotional work in Bitcoin or other cryptocurrencies as several organizations accept payment in cryptocurrencies now. For the business of every size and industry, blockchain press releases deliver exceptional results. For instance, they can work like a magic wand to grow your online presence and boost exposure.

You must first explore the ways how to use blockchain press releases to reach the wide audience not just online but also in print world. This brings a lot of business for your organization, and even if you have to invest some money on it, you should go for it. Some online portals accept blockchain press releases; you can hire their services for initial boost.

Professional Promotional Work by Blockchain Press Releases

As it has been mentioned above blockchain press releases can play important role in the entire affair of not just public relations but also branding. However, you should hire only professional blockchain press release writers as they know how to maximize the scope and reach. You can expect from a top-notch press release writing service provider that they bring impact.

Even experts admit that blockchain press releases can be a crucial marketing element for business because of the probabilities for free media coverage. Needless to say, the news release is a key weapon in the fight to make your brand get noticed by a large number of audiences. Therefore, ensure that you have the right people to work on the releases.

Benefiting from Professional Press Release Writing

As it has been mentioned above all businesses can benefit from press release distribution services; however, press releases should be written by professionals. No matter how small or big your company is and no matter what industry you are in, you can benefit from this distribution; however, the job should be done by professionals.

Needless to say, you may not have the great story to share to media, but you can still get blockchain press releases written to share online. It is easy to share press releases online and get noticed than getting the story covered by news portals or newspapers for that matter.

CHAPTER 5: BLOCKCHAIN NEWS

Over the last couple of years, the new financial technology called blockchain has emerged as a leading solution for banks, governments, and people at large. The latest blockchain news from around the world claims that this technology has produced some of the best solutions for people. For instance, Bitcoin, a product of blockchain technology is a popular cryptocurrency.

The latest blockchain news is the fact that the blockchain startups make up 20% large crowdfunding projects. This simply shows that the venture capitalists trust the potential that the blockchain has. The fact that the list of top crowdfunding campaigns is becoming increasingly blockchain dominated as of late itself gives confidence to the investors.

Blockchain can have a lot of beneficial feature for various groups of people and organizations. The concept and structure of a blockchain were first introduced to the world in the Bitcoin whitepaper in 2008. The letter was written under the pseudonym Satoshi Nakamoto who has recently disclosed his identity for the people.

Blockchain Technology Companies Flourishing

The latest and updated blockchain news claims that a blockchain is a public, distributed database of time-stamped "blocks" of transactions on its network. The reports and analysis inform that with this series of blocks, anyone can view the entire history of transactions across the ledger and come to the consensus on its current state.

Thus, there are plenty of uses of blockchain technology. Reading the latest and updated blockchain news can help them make the professional decision. Nonetheless, as the design of Satoshi's open-source Bitcoin blockchain inspired many to contribute to the code base. The news suggests that many to start working on their extensions of the software.

Blockchain News Educates People about the Futuristic Financial Technology

There are two kinds of thoughts on blockchain technology. For instance, there are those who claim blockchains as a complementary technology and then there are those who argue blockchains as an alternative technology. However, only time will be the true test as it will decide whether this has bright future or will become obsolete.

Needless to say, a lot of traders predict that depending on the industry and use case, there will be there different scenarios of how blockchain adoption plays out among enterprise companies, considering these two states. For instance, the government of Haiti has decided to use the technology to keep the land records transparent and available for the citizens.

Some blockchain events are scheduled for the next months that are going to play an important role in shaping the future of the futuristic financial technology. Needless to say, most of these events are being organized by one or more advocacy groups that are working towards safe and secure financial technology. They are playing important roles in all the development.

Notwithstanding what one such event is 'Blockchain for Wall Street.' The organizers of the blockchain event claim that the blockchain technology space has evolved rapidly during the past year. According to them, as Wall Street firms have begun to kick the tires of early software and engage in proof-of-concepts, around which much discussion has taken place.

The organizers inform that the event is scheduled for November 29th at NYC and has a busy agenda where they will discuss a range of issues. According to them the coming year will be a crucial one as firms move from PoCs to limited rollouts in production environments. The event is a day of practical education and peer-to-peer engagement.

Second Blockchain Hackathon, Dublin

This is one of the most popular blockchain events in Ireland. According to the organizers, last year was such a success; they couldn't avoid rerunning the Hackathon. This is a great opportunity on 4th to 6th November where participants as getting a weekend of learning, hacking, and building stuff. The registrations are open for interested candidates.

Notwithstanding what the best technical experts in the blockchain field will be there to help and mentor the participants. The organizers of the blockchain event claim that they are here to play with technology so no worries if participants are a newbie. They expect the event to be full-house again, with participants from all around the globe.

Finovate Asia, Scheduled for November 8, 2016, in Hong Kong

The organizers of this blockchain event claim that as the interest in the latest financial technology going up Asia can emerge as an epicenter. Regarding who can attend it, they inform that anyone with an interest or stake in the future of banking and financial technology should come to Finovate Asia.

The blockchain event according to the organizers provides an exciting opportunity for all those are responsible for developing or marketing new products, anyone who needs to keep up to date on the latest innovations in the industry, and anyone who can benefit from the opportunity to view in-depth demos from cutting-edge startups.

There are various portals that provide the latest and updated Ethereum news to readers and even traders or investors can take advantage of the same. The latest development is that Zhong An, China's first online insurance company, has established Zhong An Technology to conduct research and development on artificial intelligence, Blockchain and cloud computing.

The news reports claim that the major focus of the company is on implementing Blockchains into their online insurance platform. The Ethereum news claims that with the latest development the firm aims to be an innovator in the healthcare and finance sectors. This has been welcomed by the entire industry that thinks it can invite further investments.

Talking about the development Xing Jiang, CTO of ZhongAn said that with the creation of Zhong an Technology, they are developing a new FinTech ecosystem. They are not just integrating technological research with financial innovation but also aim to be an accelerator for both the finance and healthcare sectors.

Updated Ethereum News on the Uses of Ethereum

Ethereum has caught popular attention in very short time; the latest development in China just evidence. Needless to say, the subsidiary has already worked with more than 20 partners from Blockchain-applicable sectors. These sectors include banking, insurance, and healthcare and they all aim to create the Shanghai Blockchain Enterprise Development Alliance.

The alliance according to the various Ethereum news reports one of China's first Blockchain-focused bodies to develop Blockchain applications. Notwithstanding what Zhong an Technology has even teamed up with Fudan University's School of Computer Sciences and Technology. The two organizations aim to set up a FinTech laboratory focused on Blockchain and security.

Finding Out Latest Ethereum News for Fundamental Analysis

Like what happens in the equity market, in Ethereum trading traders go for technical and fundamental analysis so that they can make a profitable trading decision. The portals providing the latest and updated Ethereum news know the requirement and custom design the solution. In their news stories, they also bring in the fundamental analysis.

There are some portals like News BTC that provide Ethereum technical analysis where they provide coverage to the trading ideas and tell when to enter into a position and when to exit. With the help of technical and fundamental analysis traders you can make profitable trading decisions. Needless to say, Ethereum news and analysis has become fundamental for traders.

CHAPTER 6: BLOCKCHAIN INVENTION

After it emerged in 2008, the technology behind the world's most famous cryptocurrency, Bitcoin, held court on the fringes, attracting attention mostly from startups and the financial services sector. However, it has recently started to receive a lot of attention as companies gradually realize it could be valuable for many other things besides tracking payments.

Simply put, a blockchain is a distributed ledger that sorts transactions into blocks. Each block is chained to the one before it, using sophisticated math, all the way back to the first transaction. Entries are permanent, transparent, and searchable, which makes it possible for community members to view transaction histories in their entirety. Each update constitutes a new "block," added to the end of the "chain" - a structure that makes it difficult for anyone to modify the records at a later stage. The ledger allows information to be recorded and shared among large groups of unrelated companies and all members must collectively validate any updates - which is in everyone's interest.

To date, much attention and money have been spent on financial applications for the technology. However, an equally promising test case lies with global supply chain relationships, whose complexity and diversity of interests pose exactly the kinds of challenges this technology seeks to address.

A simple application of the blockchain paradigm to the supply chain could be to register the transfer of goods on the ledger.

BLOCKCHAIN

Transactions would identify the parties involved, as well as the price, date, location, quality, and state of the product and any other information that would be relevant to managing the supply chain.

The cryptography-based and immutable nature of the transactions would make it nearly impossible to compromise the ledger.

Now, a slew of startups and corporations are deploying blockchain to re-invent their global supply chain and run their businesses more efficiently:

1. For Maersk, the world's largest shipping company, the challenge is not tracking the familiar rectangular shipping containers that sail the world aboard cargo ships. Instead, it is circumnavigating the mountains of paperwork associated with each container. A single container can require stamps and approvals from as many as 30 parties, including customs, tax officials and health authorities, spread across 200 or more interactions. While containers can be loaded on a ship in a matter of minutes, a container can be held up at port for days because a piece of paper goes missing, while the goods inside spoil. The cost of moving and keeping track of all this paperwork often equals the cost of physically moving the container around the world. The system is also rife with fraud as the valuable bill of lading can be tampered with, or copied, letting criminals siphon off goods or circulate counterfeit products, leading to billions of dollars in maritime fraud each year.

Last summer, Maersk sought cooperation from customs authorities, freight forwarders and the producers that fill the containers. It began running its first trials of a new digital shipping ledger with these partners, for shipping routes between Rotterdam and Newark. After signing off on a document, the customs authorities could immediately upload a copy of it, with a digital signature, so that everyone else involved - including Maersk itself and other government authorities - could see that it was complete. If there were disputes later, everyone could go back to the record and be confident that no one had altered it in the meantime. The cryptography involved also makes it hard for the virtual signatures to be forged.

The second test tracked all of the paperwork related to a container of flowers moving from the Port of Mombasa, in Kenya, to Rotterdam, in the Netherlands. As both trials went well, Maersk followed up by tracking containers with pineapples from Colombia, and mandarin oranges from California.

2. Like most merchants, Wal-Mart struggles to identify and remove food that needs to be recalled. When a customer becomes ill, it can take weeks to identify the product, shipment, and vendor. To remedy this, it announced last year that it would start using blockchain to record and log the origins of produce - crucial data from a single receipt, including suppliers, details on how and where food was grown and who inspected it. The database extends information from the pallet to the individual package.

This gives it the ability to immediately find where a tainted product came from in a matter of minutes versus days, as well as capture other important attributes to make an informed decision around food flow.

Wal-Mart, has already completed two pilot programs - moving pork from Chinese farms to Chinese stores, and produce from Latin America to the United States - and is now confident a finished version can be put together within a few years.

3. BHP relies on vendors at nearly every stage in the mining process, contracting with geologists and shipping companies to collect samples and conduct analyses that drive business decisions involving multiple parties distributed across continents. Those vendors typically keep track of rock and fluid samples and reviews with emails and spreadsheets. A lost file can cause big and expensive headaches since the samples help the company decide where to drill new wells.

BHP's solution, which started this year, is used blockchain to record movements of wellbore rock and fluid samples and better secure the real-time data that is generated during delivery. Decentralized file storage, multi-party data acquisition, and immutability, as well as immediate accessibility, are all aspects that will enhance its supply chain.

BHP has now required its vendors to use an app to collect live data - with a dashboard and options on what to do that are very streamlined to their respective jobs. A technician taking a specimen can attach data such as collection time, a lab researcher can add reports, and all will be immediately visible to everyone who has access. No more lost samples or frantic messages. While certain elements of the process are the same, the new system is expected to drive internal efficiencies while allowing BHP to work more efficiently with its partners.

For now, in most first deployments, blockchain is running parallel with companies' current systems - often older databases or spreadsheets like Microsoft's Excel. The hardest part will be to create new business models. Deploying blockchain enterprise-wide means companies will often have to scrap their existing business processes and start from scratch. An endeavor not for the faint hearted.

The DIM Ecosystem will allow individuals and businesses to conduct state-of-the-art

Encrypted transactions, send, receive, trade, and manage company shares and assets in

Online wallets.

This will enable crypto stock trading and equity tokenization, on

Computers, mobile devices or via password-encrypted paper certificates.

DIMCOIN will host a Pre-ICO (Initial Coin Offering) starting on the 1st of July, 2017 at

12:00 CET until the 15th of July at 23:59 CET. The ICO will start on the 16th of July at

00:00 CET until the 27th of August at 23:59 CET. Each 100 DIMCOIN purchased during

The ICO will receive 1 DIM TOKEN. A total of 1.74 billion DIMCOIN, including the bonuses

And the 10 million DIM TOKEN that will be allocated for purchase by investors during the

ICO.

The DIM TOKEN gives investors holding more than 50 DIM TOKEN some unique and

Exclusive benefits within the DIM Ecosystem, which are voting rights and a percentage of

Fees. The DIM TOKEN is an opportunity to earn lifetime recurring income based on

Transactions.

Phase 1 (Pre-ICO) starts with a 30% BONUS, resulting in 1$ = 100 DIMCOIN ($ 0.01 per 1

DIMCOIN) + 30 DIMCOIN BONUS + 1 DIM TOKEN. The ICO bonus will decrease until the

End of the DIM TOKEN sale. Once the first funding goal of $10 million has been reached,

There will be a dynamic price offer of $0.02 up to $0.12 per DIMCOIN. After $30 million

Has been reached, the price offer will be locked at $0.12 until all allocated coins have

Been purchased.

The DIMCOIN will be listed and traded on the main cryptocurrency

Exchanges around the world, starting in the 4th Quarter of 2017.

DIMCOIN is built using NEM blockchain technology, which offers a unique two-tier

Design using node reputation, spam protection, and incentivized infrastructure through

Supernodes, all to ensure transparent and secure online trading and transactions.

With NEM as a foundation, DIMCOIN will revolutionize the industry of financial services and

Deliver a state-of-the-art ecosystem platform for assets and services.

CHAPTER 7: BLOCKCHAIN REMITTANCE

Blockchain remittance

When it comes to remittance, also known as the process of sending a certain amount of money as payment, technology has been working to change the process into something that is easier, cheaper, and faster than it ever has been thanks to electronic processes now available.

More than ever, it's has become important to find a solution for global remittance as more companies and individuals want to more money between countries.

Enter blockchain. Blockchain is an important technology set to completely improve the remittance system and potentially replace what has been a cumbersome bank settlement system.

The old system with the banks has been bogged down, especially because they insist on too many steps and they are laden with costs that are designed to prevent fraud. Blockchain's public ledger is creating a new payment network that can help businesses.

Here's what you need to know about blockchain for remittance, also now being labeled as "remittance" services:

No high transfer costs: Blockchain is set to lower the transfer costs of global remittance, including bank and fraud prevention fees. Add exchange rates and the fees to do currency exchange on both ends of the remittance and a traditional remittance transaction can quickly get expensive. However, none of these fees come into effect when using a blockchain remittance process.

Simplified experience: Blockchain offers a straightforward remittance process thanks to the removal of multiple steps in the payment process. Since there are fewer people and processes involved, there is nothing complex about blockchain remittance. It follows a basic and proven transaction formula that has worked for other type of payment processing already as well as for non-financial transactions.

Speed: With blockchain the transfer of money, is nearly instantaneous. This means that there will be no more five to seven business day averages with remittance. Blockchain provides the ability to move money at this rate, and can then speed up productivity in terms of what businesses and individuals can accomplish with that extra time. Plus, that level of speed can be a game changer when it comes to cash flow, helping businesses of all sizes and individuals to have greater control over their money and expenses.

No middleman: While traditional remittance measures require a third-party that handles the authorization and release of the payment, blockchain removes this middleman. This decentralized structure to the entire process is one of the primary reasons the remittance process goes faster and costs less.

Security measures: Blockchain offers an anti-fraud feature that makes it more difficult for hackers to break into transactions as well as features that prevent any access to payment data. Any security issues have been found to primarily relate to user error and have the ability to be fixed. Easily. Other security measures have been related primarily to the overall development and maturity of blockchain and how it can be used.

Privacy and anonymity: While the ability to protect privacy and provide anonymity is a benefit to many businesses and organizations, there is concern with regulators and governments related to concerns over terrorists and criminals using it to move their money around the world. This is an ongoing issue that countries and regulators are exploring to see if there is a solution that will maintain privacy while not enabling criminals to take advantage of blockchain remittance.

Still in its infancy: Blockchain for remittance is still in its trial stages in many countries so there is a ways to go before it becomes a common household word and a way to transfer money on a global basis. Many organizations are still reluctant because they are not sure if the world will agree to eventually forego traditional currency and cash for the digital currency that is used for blockchain-based remittance. Because this is a new way of looking at payments and money, more creative thinking and perspective are important by those within the financial industry as well as with businesses that will eventually adopt this type of remittance process. Despite the ongoing development, acceptance is growing as more blockchain companies emerge to illustrate how it can be used.

Best served in underdeveloped markets: Blockchain is viewed as opening the door to working with underdeveloped markets, particularly those in Africa as well as in countries throughout Asia. With no real legacy infrastructure in place, it's been difficult for businesses in these countries to join the global business environment, let alone conduct transactions in their own countries. The World Bank noted that India had $69 billion in remittances in 2015 while China had $64 billion, the Philippines had $28 billion, Mexico had $25 billion, and Nigeria had $21 billion. As the World

Bank noted, "Remittances are an important and fairly stable source of income for millions of families and of foreign exchange to many developing However, if remittances continue to slow, and dramatically as in the case of Central Asian countries, poor families in many parts of the world would face serious challenges including nutrition, access to health care and education." Blockchain provides the ability for cross border remittance products, which are in considerable demand as noted in the aforementioned statistics, and could significantly grow this market opportunity.

There's so much happening in the world of blockchain and cryptocurrency, making it an exciting time to be operating within a realm that requires any type of transaction. There will continue to be evolution with blockchain across all types of applications, including remittance, which will help businesses and individuals access more options related to sending and receiving money anywhere in the world.

Using Blockchain to Enable Faster Cross Border Remittance

Fintech as a whole is rapidly adopting potential applications of the blockchain across the board and many players in the space seem keen to test out what efficiencies can be extracted out of this emerging technology in the fastest and most disruptive way possible. It's clear that there is much room for growth in the space of remittances using distributed ledger technology.

Existing Remittance Options Take Too Long

Currently, anyone who banks with major institutions knows what's involved, at least on the user end, with remitting money overseas.

First off, it takes a lot of time. When you transfer funds between SWIFT affiliated banks, some institutions take can take up to five days or more. In the case of needing an instant solution to take the place of this, blockchain technology is a useful one. Cryptocurrencies which are already proven on blockchain technology can transfer funds with a state of security within minutes.

Remitting Funds Cross-Border Is Expensive

The second problem with cross-border remittance is that the cost can be restrictive. Blockchain remittances are cheaper and more secure for both financial bodies and end users due to the simple yet extraordinary networking technology which cuts out time and fees. For people within developed nations who send money to their families overseas, the fees with traditional banks can tumble up to hundreds of dollars, often being charged both to send and receive funds. For those in developing countries, the need for low-cost remittances is even greater. In countries such as the Nigeria and the Philippines, remittances form a huge fraction of their GDP, around 4% and 10% respectively. Every dollar spent on the fees associated with sending the money is likely better used elsewhere.

Opening Up Options To Those Who Need Them

Lastly, the access to traditional banking solutions within developing nations can be a major issue for people to overcome in their attempts to transfer money. Even if banks systems are available, not everyone has access to them. Having a more widely spread solution based on blockchain technology takes the nearly exclusive power that mega-banks have over cross-border remittances and gives more opportunities to people who need them.

Blockchain technology gives us the power to change and radically improve on efficiencies in many tried and true industries that we just take for granted as being big, slow, complex, but ultimately reliable. When we add in forefront industry expertise with blockchain technology, amazing new innovations are possible that will help people all over the world with not only revolutionary new features and abilities, but more reliability and transparency in the process.

CHAPTER 8: BLOCKCHAIN SOFTWARE

Blockchain technology has a large potential to transform business operating models in the long term. Blockchain distributed ledger technology is more a foundational technology — with the potential to create new foundations for global economic and social systems — than a disruptive technology, which typically "attack a traditional business model with a lower-cost solution and overtake incumbent firms quickly. Even so, a few operational products are maturing from proof of concept by late 2016. The use of blockchains promises to bring significant efficiencies to global supply chains, financial transactions, and asset ledgers and decentralized social networking.

Blockchains technology can be integrated into multiple areas. This means specific blockchain applications may be a disruptive innovation because substantially lower-cost solutions can be instantiated, which can disrupt existing business models. Blockchain protocols facilitate businesses to use new methods of processing digital transactions. Examples include a payment system and digital currency, facilitating crowd sales, or implementing prediction markets and generic governance tools. Blockchains are expected to disrupt the cloud computing industry although practical technical issues remain as obstacles. Better source needed.

Blockchains can be thought of as an automatically notarized ledger. They alleviate the need for a trust service provider and are predicted to result in less capital being tied up in disputes. Blockchains have the potential to reduce systemic risk and financial fraud. They automate processes that were previously time-consuming and done manually, such as the incorporation of businesses] in theory, it would be possible to collect taxes, conduct conveyancing and provide risk management with blockchains.

Major applications of blockchain include cryptocurrencies— including Bitcoin, BlackCoin, Dash, and Nxt—and blockchain platforms such as Factor as a distributed registry, Gems for decentralized messaging, MaidSafe for decentralized applications, Store for a distributed cloud, and Texas for decentralized voting. Each cryptocurrency has its features and particularities.

Frameworks and trials such as the one at the Sweden Land Registry aim to demonstrate the effectiveness of the blockchain at speeding land sale deals. The Republic of Georgia is piloting a blockchain-based property registry. The Ethical and Fair Creators Association uses blockchain to help startups protect their authentic ideas.

New distribution methods are available for the insurance industry such as peer-to-peer insurance, parametric insurance, and micro insurance following the adoption of the blockchain. Banks are interested in this technology because it has potential to speed up back office settlement systems. The sharing economy and IoT are also set to benefit from blockchains because they involve many collaborating peers. Online voting is another application of the blockchain. Blockchains are being used to develop information systems for medical records, which increases interoperability. In theory, legacy disparate systems can be completely replaced by blockchains. Blockchains are being developed for data storage, publishing texts and identifying the origin of digital art.

Banks such as UBS are opening new research labs dedicated to blockchain technology to explore how blockchain can be used in financial services to increase efficiency and reduce costs.

BLOCKCHAIN

A blockchain facilitates secure online transactions through decentralized and distributed digital ledger that is used to record transactions across many computers so that the record cannot be altered retroactively without the alteration of all subsequent blocks and the collusion of the network.

This allows the participants to verify and audit transactions inexpensively. They are authenticated by mass collaboration powered by collective self-interests. The result is a robust workflow where participants' uncertainty regarding data security is marginal. The use of a blockchain removes the characteristic of infinite reproducibility from a digital asset. It confirms that each unit of value was transferred only once, solving the long-standing problem of double spending. Blockchains have been described as a value-exchange protocol. This blockchain-based exchange of value can be completed more quickly, more safely and more cheaply than with traditional systems A blockchain can assign title rights because it provides a record that compels offer and acceptance.

A blockchain database consists of two kinds of records: transactions and blocks. Blocks hold batches of valid transactions that are hashed and encoded into a Merkle tree. Each block includes the hash of the prior block in the blockchain, linking the two. Variants of this format were used previously, for example in Git. The format is not by itself sufficient to qualify as a blockchain. The linked blocks form a chain.

Sometimes separate blocks can be produced concurrently, creating a temporary fork. In addition to a secure hash based history, any blockchain has a specified algorithm for scoring different versions of the history so that one with a higher value can be selected over others. Blocks not selected for inclusion in the chain are called orphan blocks.

Peers supporting the database don't have the same version of the history at all times. Instead, they keep the highest scoring version of the database that they currently know of. Whenever a peer receives a higher scoring version (usually the old version with a single new block added) they extend or overwrite their database and retransmit the improvement to their peers. There is never an absolute guarantee that any particular entry will remain in the best version of the history forever.

Because blockchains are typically built to add the score of new blocks onto old blocks and because there are incentives to work only on extending with new blocks rather than overwriting old blocks, the probability of an entry becoming superseded goes down exponentially as more blocks are built on top of it, eventually becoming very low.

For example, in a blockchain, using the proof-of-work system, the chain with the most cumulative proof-of-work is always considered the valid one by the network. Some methods can be used to demonstrate a sufficient level of computation. Within a blockchain, the computation is carried out redundantly rather than in the traditional segregated and parallel manner

Blockchain is essentially a database, a giant network, known as a distributed ledger, which records ownership and value, and allows anyone with access to view and take part. A network is updated and verified through consensus of all the parties involved. When something is added it cannot be altered and, if it looks valid to everyone, the update is approved.

BLOCKCHAIN

The first generation brought the internet of information. The second generation, powered by blockchain, is bringing us the internet of value, a new, distributed platform that can help us reshape the world of business and transform the old order of human affairs for the better. But like the internet in the late-1980s and early-1990s, this is still early days."

Blockchain, a distributed ledger, is an asset database that can be shared across a network of multiple sites, geographies or institutions. All participants within a network can have their own identical copy of the ledger. Any changes to the ledger are reflected in all copies, similar to a Google doc. On the other hand, a centralized asset ledger, or clearing house, the model currently used by financial services globally, is a list of transactions that is controlled by a single entity.

As early as 1981, inventors were attempting to solve the Internet's problems of privacy, security, and inclusion with cryptography. No matter how they reengineered the process, there were always leaks because third parties were involved. Paying with credit cards over the Internet was insecure because users had to divulge too much personal data, and the transaction fees were too high for small payments.

A decade later in 2008, the global financial industry crashed. Perhaps propitiously, the pseudonymous Satoshi Nakamoto–who may or may not be an Australian entrepreneur named Craig Wright–outlined a new protocol for a peer-to-peer electronic cash system using a cryptocurrency, or digital currency, called Bitcoin. Cryptocurrencies are different from traditional fiat currencies because they are not created or controlled by countries. This protocol established a set of rules — in the form of distributed computations—that ensured the integrity of the data exchanged among these billions of devices without going through a trusted third party. This seemingly subtle act set off a spark that has excited, terrified, or otherwise captured the imagination of the computing world and has spread like wildfire everywhere.

"They're like, 'Oh my god, this is it. This is the big breakthrough,'" said Marc Andreessen, the co-creator of the first commercial Web browser Netscape, and a big investor in technology ventures. "This is the distributed trust network that the Internet always needed and never had."

Today thoughtful people everywhere are trying to understand the implications of a protocol that enables mere mortals to manufacture trust through clever code. This has never happened before—trusted transactions directly between two or more parties, authenticated by mass collaboration and powered by collective self-interests, rather than by large corporations motivated by profit.

It may not be the Almighty, but a trustworthy global platform for our transactions is something very big. We're calling it the Trust Protocol.

This protocol is the foundation of a growing number of global distributed ledgers called blockchains—of which the Bitcoin blockchain is the largest. While the technology is complicated, the main idea is simple. Blockchains enable us to send money directly and safely from me to you, without going through a bank, a credit card company, or PayPal.

Rather than the Internet of Information, it's the Internet of Value or of Money. It's also a platform for everyone to know what is true—

at least with regard to structured recorded information. At its most basic, it is an open source code: anyone can download it for free, run it, and use it to develop new tools for managing transactions online. As such, it holds the potential for unleashing countless new applications and as yet unrealized capabilities that have the potential to transform many things they work.

Bitcoin or other digital currency isn't saved in a file somewhere; it's represented by transactions recorded in a blockchain—kind of like a global spreadsheet or ledger, which leverages the resources of a large peer-to-peer bitcoin network to verify and approve each Bitcoin transaction. Each blockchain, like the one that uses Bitcoin, is distributed: it runs on computers by volunteers around the world; there is no central database to hack. The blockchain is public: anyone can view it at any time because it resides on the network, not within a single institution charged with auditing transactions and keeping records. And the blockchain is encrypted: it uses heavy-duty encryption involving public and private keys–like the two-key system to access a safety deposit box–to maintain virtual security.

Every 10 minutes, all the transactions conducted are verified, cleared and stored in a block that is linked to the preceding block, creating a chain. Each block must refer to the preceding block to be valid. This structure permanently time-stamps and stores exchanges of value, preventing anyone from altering the ledger. If you wanted to steal a Bitcoin, you'd have to rewrite the coin's entire history on the blockchain in broad daylight. That's practically impossible. So the blockchain is a distributed ledger representing a network consensus of every transaction that has ever occurred. Like the World Wide Web of information, it's the World Wide Ledger of value — a distributed ledger that everyone can download and run on their personal computer.

Some scholars have argued that the invention of double-entry bookkeeping enabled the rise of capitalism and the nation-state. This new digital ledger of economic transactions can be programmed to record virtually everything of value and importance to humankind: birth and death certificates, deeds and titles of ownership, financial accounts, votes, provenance of food, and anything else that can be expressed in code.

The new platform enables a reconciliation of digital records regarding just about everything in real time. In fact, soon billions of smart things in the physical world will be sensing, responding, communicating, sharing important data, doing everything from protecting our environment to managing our health. This Internet of Everything needs a Ledger of Everything. Business, commerce, and the economy need a Digital Reckoning.

So why should you care? We believe the truth can set us free and distributed trust will profoundly affect people in all walks of life. Maybe you're a consumer who wants to know where that hamburger meat really came from. Perhaps you're an immigrant who's sick of paying big fees to send money home to loved ones. Maybe you're an aid worker who needs to identify land titles of landowners so you can rebuild their homes after an earthquake. Or a citizen fed up with the lack of transparency and accountability of political leaders. Or a user of social media who values your privacy and thinks all the data you generate might be worth something — to you. Even as we write,

BLOCKCHAIN

Without Lamport et al.'s pioneering work in the field of distributed computing and distributed algorithms, we would not be contemplating the possibilities offered by blockchain technology today. The most widely known application of this technology so far is attributed to Satoshi Nakamoto. Blockchain's boom as an application for things such as value calculation, currency exchange, data storage in the cloud, or contracts, has received widespread attention in subsequent years. Blockchain technology's potential in developments such as the Internet of Things, (mobile) health care and advanced manufacturing has only been attracting increasing interest in the past two years.

A recent Deloitte publication described blockchain technology as: "a new solution to a more challenging version of the Byzantine Generals problem that includes the ability to add participants over time. A blockchain is a digital distributed transaction ledger, with identical copies maintained on multiple computer systems controlled by different entities". Melanie Swan sees blockchain technology as a key innovation in the development of new architectures for transactions between interconnected and distributed systems: "The blockchain allows the disintermediation and decentralization of all transactions of any type between all parties on a global basis". To Swan, decentralized ledgers that enable a transparent structure of recorded transactions are the essence of the blockchain: "the database that is shared by all network nodes, updated by miners, monitored by everyone and owned and controlled by no one". Physical nodes in a network, such as computers, smartphones, sensors and devices such as smart TVs, fridges and cars can thus be interconnected through software and distributed algorithms that ensure consensus in transactions between these nodes. In Swan's words, the blocks that make up the blockchain consist of: "groups of transactions posted sequentially to the ledger - that is, added to the chain. Blockchain ledgers can be inspected publicly with block explorers, internet sites where you can see a transactions stream by entering a blockchain address (a user's public-key address)".

Distributed computing, Blockchain and the IoT

Many agree that Bitcoin is but a first step towards numerous more applications in a wide range of sectors. A Goldman Sachs publication cited by Williams-Grut claims that: "While the Bitcoin hype cycle has gone quiet, Silicon Valley and Wall Street are betting that the underlying technology behind it, the Blockchain, can change... well everything". Silicon Valley's role in developing and shaping blockchain technology is considerable. Insights such as the Byzantine Generals' Problem and the Paxos algorithm have played a major part in the development of solutions such as cloud computing and cloud-based data storage. It is therefore no surprise that Google, Microsoft and Amazon stand to gain a great deal from further development of the concept of distributed computing. Philips Healthcare has recently also announced that it is to research the potential uses of blockchain technology in exchanging and sharing data and information between medical applications. Working closely together with parties such as Samsung, IBM is investing considerable time and money into making a blockchain possible for the Internet of Things. In IBM's view, the basis of today's information revolution lies in: "the very humble work of transaction processing. From IBM expects the current growth of automated transactions to snowball on the back of the development of the Internet of Things and advanced manufacturing. According to IBM, the exponential growth of the number of objects that are connected to the internet and share information through that connection calls for new paradigms such as the blockchain of distributed computing. In the further development of a decentralized Internet of Things, IBM sees the blockchain as: "the framework facilitating transaction processing and coordination among interacting devices. Each manages its own roles and behavior, resulting in an Internet of Decentralized, Autonomous Things - and thus the democratization of the digital world".

Advantages of blockchain

Healthcare

Using digital signatures on blockchain-based data that allows access only when authorized by multiple people could regulate the availability and maintain the privacy of health records. In addition, a community of people, including hospitals, doctors, patients, and insurance companies, could be part of the overall blockchain, reducing fraud in healthcare payments.

Defense

Unauthorized access or modification of critical defense infrastructure, such as operating systems and network firmware, could seriously compromise national security. For most countries, defense infrastructure and computer systems are distributed across different locations. Blockchain technology distributed across multiple data centers can ensure security against attacks on important network and hardware equipment by ensuring consensus-based access for modification.

Government

Government departments that work in silos cause the exchange of information to be delayed, negatively impacting citizen services. Linking the data between the departments with blockchain ensures that data is released in real time, when both the departments and the citizen consent to sharing data. Blockchain technology could improve transparency and check corruption in governments worldwide.

Law

Blockchains can contain a huge amount of data, including entire contracts. The impact of "smart contracts" — protocols that facilitate or enforce contract performance using blockchain — will have a profound impact for industries. Smart contracts eliminate the middleman, such as a legal firm, as payment will happen based on certain milestones being met. By its very nature, the smart contract is easily enforceable electronically, creating a powerful escrow by taking it out of the control of a single party.

Energy

Micro generation of electricity is becoming a huge trend in the power generation business. New energy initiatives such as home power generation and community solar power are filling in gaps of power supply across the world. As micro generation adds to traditional power suppliers, it fosters creation of an energy market. Smart meters can register produced and consumed electricity in a blockchain, which allows for consumption of the surplus energy in a different location, providing credits or currency to the original producer. The credits can then be redeemed against the grid when the micro generator needs additional electricity from the grid. The blockchain enforces these contracts in real time or near-real time, allowing for a utility market to be created with minimal red tape.

With such wide-ranging possibilities, there is no surprise that blockchain has the potential to enhance the quality of service delivery while improving confidentiality and integrity of data. With its promise of providing secure and transparent transactions, blockchain seems poised to be one of the digital world's key pillars.

Transparency and immutability

Changes to public blockchains are publicly viewable by all parties creating transparency, and all transactions are immutable, meaning they cannot be altered or deleted.

Ecosystem simplification

With all transactions being added to a single public ledger, it reduces the clutter and complications of multiple ledgers.

Faster transactions

Interbank transactions can potentially take days for clearing and final settlement, especially outside of working hours. Blockchain transactions can reduce transaction times to minutes and are processed 24/7.

Lower transaction costs

By eliminating third party intermediaries and overhead costs for exchanging asset blockchains have the potential to greatly reduce transaction fees.

Disintermediation

The core value of a blockchain is enabling a database to be directly shared across boundaries of trust, without requiring a central administrator. This is possible because blockchain transactions contain their own proof of validity and their own proof of authorization, instead of requiring some centralized application logic to enforce those constraints. Transactions can therefore be verified and processed independently by multiple "nodes", with the blockchain acting as a consensus mechanism to ensure those nodes stay in sync.

Why is there value in this disintermediation? Because even though a database is just bits and bytes, it is also a tangible thing. The contents of a database are stored in the memory and disk of a particular computer system, and anybody with sufficient access to that system can destroy or corrupt the data within. As a result, the moment you entrust your data to a regular database, you also become dependent on the human organization in which that database resides.

Now, the world is filled with organizations which have earned this trust – governments and banks (mostly), universities, trade associations, and even private companies like Google and Facebook. In most cases, especially in the developed world, these work extremely well. I believe my vote has always been counted, no bank has ever stolen my money, and I'm yet to find a way to pay for better grades. So what's the problem? If an organization controls an important database, it also needs a bunch of people and processes in place to prevent that database being tampered with. People need hiring, processes need to be designed, and all this takes a great deal of time and money.

So blockchains offer a way to replace these organizations with a distributed database, locked down by clever cryptography. Like so much that has come before, they leverage the ever-increasing capacity of computer systems to provide a new way of replacing humans with code. And once it's been written and debugged, code tends to be an awful lot cheaper.

Confidentiality

As I mentioned, every node in a blockchain independently verifies and processes every transaction. A node can do this because it has full visibility into: (a) the database's current state, (b) the modification requested by a transaction, and (c) a digital signature which proves the transaction's origin. This is undoubtedly a clever new way to architect a database, and it really works. So where's the catch? For many applications, especially financial, the full transparency enjoyed by every node is an absolute deal-killer.

How do systems built on regular databases avoid this problem? Just like blockchains, they restrict the transactions that particular users can perform, but these restrictions are imposed in one central location. As a result, the full database contents need only be visible at that location, rather than in multiple nodes. Requests to read data also go through this central authority, which can accept or reject those requests as it sees fit. In other words, if a regular database is read-controlled and write-controlled, a blockchain can be write-controlled only.

To be fair, many strategies are available for mitigating this problem. These range from simple ideas like transacting under multiple blockchain addresses, to advanced cryptographic techniques such as confidential transactions and zero-knowledge proofs (now being developed). Nonetheless, the more information you want to hide on a blockchain, the heavier a computational burden you pay to generate and verify transactions. And no matter how these techniques develop, they will never beat the simple and straightforward method of hiding data completely.

Robustness

A second benefit of blockchain-powered databases is extreme fault tolerance, which stems from their built-in redundancy. Every node processes every transaction, so no individual node is crucial to the database as a whole. Similarly, nodes connect to each other in a dense peer-to-peer fashion, so many communication links can fail before things grind to a halt. The blockchain ensures that nodes which went down can always catch up on transactions they missed.

So while it's true that regular databases offer many techniques for replication, blockchains take this to a whole new level. For a start, no configuration is required – simply connect some blockchain nodes together, and they automatically keep themselves in sync. In addition, nodes can be freely added or removed from a network, without any preparation or consequences. Lastly, external users can send their transactions to any node, or to multiple nodes simultaneously, and these transactions propagate automatically and seamlessly to everyone else.

This robustness transforms the economics of database availability. With regular databases, high availability is achieved through a combination of expensive infrastructure and disaster recovery. A primary database runs on high-end hardware which is monitored closely for problems, with transactions replicated to a backup system in a different physical location. If the primary database fails (e.g. due to a power cut or catastrophic hardware failure), activity is automatically moved over to the backup, which becomes the new primary. Once the failed system is fixed, it's lined up to act as the new backup if and when necessary. While all this is doable, it's expensive and notoriously difficult to get right.

Instead, what if we had 10 blockchain nodes running in different parts of the world, all on commodity hardware? These nodes would be densely connected to each other, sharing transactions on a peer-to-peer basis and using a blockchain to ensure consensus. End users generating the transactions connect to (say) 5 of these nodes, so it doesn't matter if a few communication links go down. And if one or two nodes fail completely on any given day, nobody feels a thing, because there are still more than enough copies to go round. As it happens, this combination of low cost systems and high redundancy is exactly how Google built its search engine so cheaply. Blockchains can do the same thing for databases.

Performance

Blockchains will always be slower than centralized databases. It's not just that today's blockchains are slow because the technology is new and optimized, but it's a result of the nature of blockchains themselves. You see, when processing transactions, a blockchain has to do all the same things as a regular database, but it carries three additional burdens:

Signature verification. Every blockchain transaction must be digitally signed using a public-private cryptography scheme such as ECDSA. This is necessary because transactions propagate between nodes in a peer-to-peer fashion, so their source cannot otherwise be proven. The generation and verification of these signatures is computationally complex, and constitutes the primary bottleneck in products like ours. By contrast, in centralized databases, once a connection has been established, there is no need to individually verify every request that comes over it.

Consensus mechanisms. In a distributed database such as a blockchain, effort must be expended in ensuring that nodes in the network reach consensus. Depending on the consensus mechanism used, this might involve significant back-and-forth communication and/or dealing with forks and their consequent rollbacks. While it's true that centralized databases must also contend with conflicting and aborted transactions, these are far less likely where transactions are queued and processed in a single location.

Redundancy. This isn't about the performance of an individual node, but the total amount of computation that a blockchain requires. Whereas centralized databases process transactions once (or twice), in a blockchain they must be processed independently by every node in the network. So lots more work is being done for the same end result.

DISADVANTAGES OF BLOCKCHAIN

PERFORMANCE

Because of the nature of blockchains, it will always be slower than centralized databases. When a transaction is being processed, a blockchain has to do all the same things just like a regular database does, but it carries three additional burdens as well:

Signature verification. Every blockchain transaction must be digitally signed using a public-private cryptography scheme such as ECDSA. This is necessary because transactions propagate between nodes in a peer-to-peer fashion, so their source cannot otherwise be proven. The generation and verification of these signatures are computationally complex, and constitutes the primary bottleneck in products like ours. By contrast, in centralized databases, once a connection has been established, there is no need to individually verify every request that comes over it.

Consensus mechanisms. In a distributed database such as a blockchain, effort must be expended in ensuring that nodes in the network reach consensus. Depending on the consensus mechanism used, this might involve significant back-and-forth communication and/or dealing with forks and their consequent rollbacks. While it's true that centralized databases must also contend with conflicting and aborted transactions, these are far less likely where transactions are queued and processed in a single location.

Redundancy. This isn't about the performance of an individual node, but the total amount of computation that a blockchain requires. Whereas centralized databases process transactions once (or twice), in a blockchain they must be processed independently by every node in the network. So lots more work is being done for the same end result.

www.ingramcontent.com/pod-product-compliance
Lightning Source LLC
Chambersburg PA
CBHW050018230526
45470CB00003B/1027